ANDREW YORK'S

JAZZ GUITAR FOR CLASSICAL CATS

Chord/ Melody

Approved Curriculum

The Classical Guitarist's Guide to Jazz

Alfred, the leader in educational publishing, and the National Guitar Workshop, one of America's finest guitar schools, have joined forces to bring you the best, most progressive educational tools possible. We hope you will enjoy this book and encourage you to look for other fine products from Alfred and the National Guitar Workshop.

This book was acquired, edited and produced by Workshop Arts, Inc., the publishing arm of the National Guitar Workshop.

Nathaniel Gunod, editor

Michael Rodman, editor

Gary Tomassetti, music typesetter and assistant editor

Timothy Phelps, interior design

Linda Parnell, cover/interior line art

The CD was recorded at Studio 9, Pomona, CA and mastered at Bar None Studios, Northford, CT

Cover art: Juan Gris, Spanish, 1887–1927
Le Canigou, 1921
oil on canvas
25 1/2 x 39 1/2" (unframed)   34 3/4 x 48 5/8 x 2 3/4" (framed)
Room of Contemporary Art Fund, 1947
RCA 1947:5
Albright-Knox Art Gallery, Buffalo, New York

ISBN 0-7390-0920-6 (Book)
ISBN 0-7390-0921-4 (Book & CD)
ISBN 0-7390-0922-2 (CD)

NATIONAL GUITAR WORKSHOP

Alfred

Edited by Nathaniel Gunod

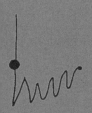

TABLE OF CONTENTS

The CD that is available for this book can make learning with the book easier
and more enjoyable. It includes performances by Andrew York. The symbol
shown above will appear next to every example and piece that is on the CD.
Use the CD to ensure that you are capturing the feel of the examples,
interpreting the rhythms correctly, and so on.
The track numbers below the symbols correspond directly to the example you
want to hear. Track 1 will help you tune your guitar to this CD.

HAVE FUN!

ABOUT THE AUTHOR

Andrew York presents a unique persona in the world of guitar. He is well known to classical guitarists through the recordings of his compositions by John Williams, Christopher Parkening and himself; and in the fingerstyle world for his inclusion on the extremely popular Windham Hill Records "Guitar Sampler." Few guitarists cross over stylistic boundaries with such authority and depth of writing and playing. Andrew's second CD, "Denouement," on GSP Recordings, won the 1994 *Guitar Player* reader's poll for best classical guitar album. The Rhino Records release "Legends of Guitar — Classical," featuring such luminaries as Segovia, Julian Bream and Los Romeros, also includes Andrew playing his composition *Sunburst*. Andrew York is also a member of the world-renowned Los Angeles Guitar Quartet. The quartet also performs and records Andrew's compositions written specifically for the group.

PHOTO · STEVEN ATHA

INTRODUCTION

What is chord/melody? Basically, it is playing a melody and the harmonizing chords at the same time. In a way, playing a classical guitar piece is playing chord/melody, because everything is there, melody and harmony—it is complete. But in jazz, chord/melody usually means a setting of a standard, well-known song. These standards are learned by jazz players as part of the traditional repertoire; at a gig any one of these tunes can be called and everybody will know it, both chords and melody.

For guitar players, playing these standards with melody and harmony at the same time has become known as *chord/melody* style. The aim of this book is to cover the skills needed to play chord/melody. You'll find examples that are in the style of some of the jazz standards (the standards themselves won't be used because of copyright restrictions), as well as exercises and multiple harmonic settings of melodies.

This book presupposes that you have a functional grasp of harmony, and an understanding of jazz harmony. For a review of jazz harmony, go through the first book in this series, *Jazz Guitar for Classical Cats: Harmony* if you haven't already done so.

This book also makes the assumption that you can read music, and have a functional right- and left-hand fingerstyle technique. TAB is not used, though many of the notation examples also include chord diagram boxes for help with visualization of chord shapes.

I hope you enjoy this book and learn lots.

EDITOR'S PREFACE

This book is the second installment in a three-part series. The first book in the series, *Jazz for Classical Cats: Harmony*, was released in 1999. It explains the basics of jazz harmony such as reading jazz charts, dominant chords (extensions and alterations), ii–V progressions, various chord voicings, the blues, secondary dominants and so on.

The purpose of this book is to put that and new information to work in a chord/melody context, which, as the author points out, will be the most familiar jazz style to classical and other fingerstyle guitarists. An inquisitive, self-motivated classical or fingerstyle guitarist will be able to use this book as a jumping-off point and enjoy a lifetime of music making in this style. It's fun, and having this set of skills will help working guitarists fill out their sets on the gig.

The next book in the series, *Jazz for Classical Cats: Improvisation* will follow this book with a detailed look at improvisation. This may very well be the most exciting book in the series for us classical guitarists, because it is the area we typically know the least about. Even if we never perform as jazz guitarists, the impulse behind the spontaneous creation of music is one that we need to experience and try to bring to all of our interpretations of the classical repertoire. The joy and freedom of expression that is available in the jazz context is what attracts many of us to learning all we can about this great art form, and hopefully, to the direction of such a fine player, composer and jazz man as Andrew York.

CHAPTER ONE

Triads

First Word

The ability to play chord/melody is not something that just happens; you have to work at it. Specifically, you have to act as an arranger and work out good-sounding sequences and practice at finding good voicings. When you come up with voicings and sequences you like, then you need to make yourself use them so they become part of your chord/melody vocabulary. Arrange, experiment and spend time doing the work and you'll make continuous progress.

Not all tunes lend themselves to chord/melody arrangements. Even though I've used a couple of classical examples in this book, many historic classical pieces don't work well because:

- The harmony is rather simple and sounds forced or peculiar when extended in a jazz style
- The melodies rarely employ color tones, which are frequently used in the melodies of jazzier tunes.

Even so, the chord/melody of *Romanza* and *Greensleeves* settings included in this book will give you an idea of what is possible if you stretch a classical piece a bit.

Some chord/melody will seem hard for the left hand. If you think about it a bit differently, though, it isn't so difficult. In a swing style, some notes are "ghosted" a bit through the use of left-hand staccato. Using the left hand to articulate instead of the right is the trick; you simply lift the left-hand finger off the string to shorten the note instead of damping with the right-hand fingers. This left-hand staccato helps in two ways:

1) It allows more time to make difficult fingering changes
2) it often provides a good rhythmic feel in a jazz context

Though there are many cases in classical guitar repertoire when you wouldn't want to use this technique, in jazz this is often used and it sounds good. You may have noticed that even very good classical players often sound stiff when playing jazz arrangements; this is part of what I am talking about. If you have the CD that is available for this book, listen to how I play the examples and notice how it differs from a standard classical approach.

Enough talk. Time to dig in!

Minor Triads in Closed Voicing

Just like the jazz comping covered in the harmony book, chord/melody requires a good knowledge of harmony and a strong sense of where chord shapes are on the fingerboard. Let's begin with major and minor triads.

We'll start with an A Minor triad in *closed voicing* (a voicing is an arrangement of chord tones). Closed voicing means the notes of the chord are as close together as possible. We'll use all three inversions:

A Minor
Root Position   1st Inversion   2nd Inversion

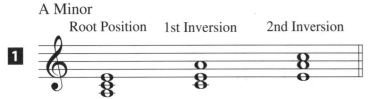

Root Position	=	Root in the bass
1st Inversion	=	3rd in the bass
2nd Inversion	=	5th in the bass

ACE, CEA, EAC

We want to be able to play A Minor triads anywhere on the fingerboard. To help you learn to visualize the triads on the fingerboard, I've written the exercise in example 2 (below). I've put the chord diagram above the notes, because seeing geometric shapes of the triads helps you to learn the finger patterns more quickly.

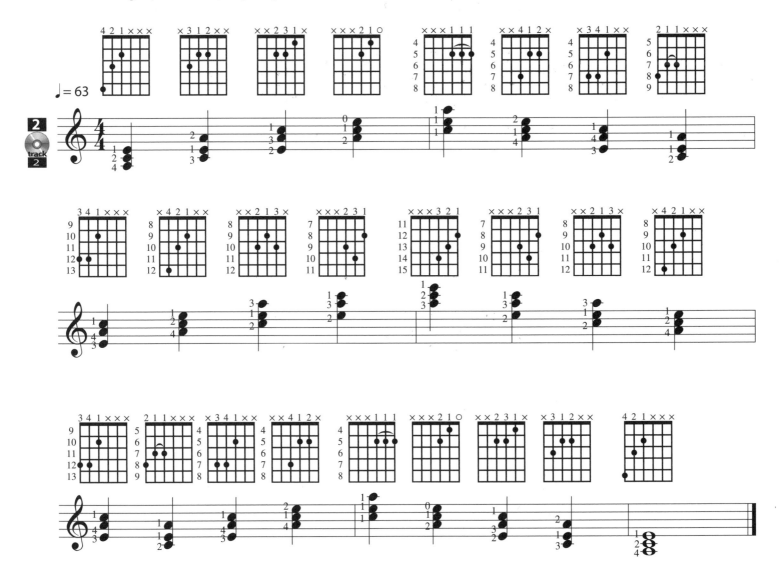

Study example 2 on page 6 until you know the finger patterns very well. Remember, we aren't trying to learn this in the "classical" way; the point is not just to be able to play these triads at a particular tempo. The goal is to *understand the relationships* between the shapes, and to see them as frozen points of a giant A Minor chord covering the entire fingerboard. Take your time—it's not the performance that counts at this point, but the depth of knowledge. The more patterns you can see, the stronger musician/player you'll be.

Another thing to keep in mind is to finger only what you need for each triad. Don't use extraneous fingers, even if the next chord will use one or all of them. Get to know each triad shape individually.

EXTRA STUDY:

Try and play example 2 using A Major triads instead of A Minor. Just change all the C♮s to C♯s.

A C♯ E, C♯ E A, E A C♯

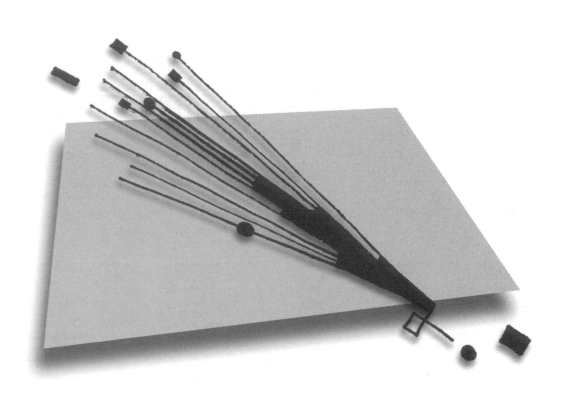

A Triad Tune

Using some of these A Minor triads and tossing in G Major triads to make it more interesting, I've written a little Chilean style tune to help you practice these triad patterns. Enjoy!

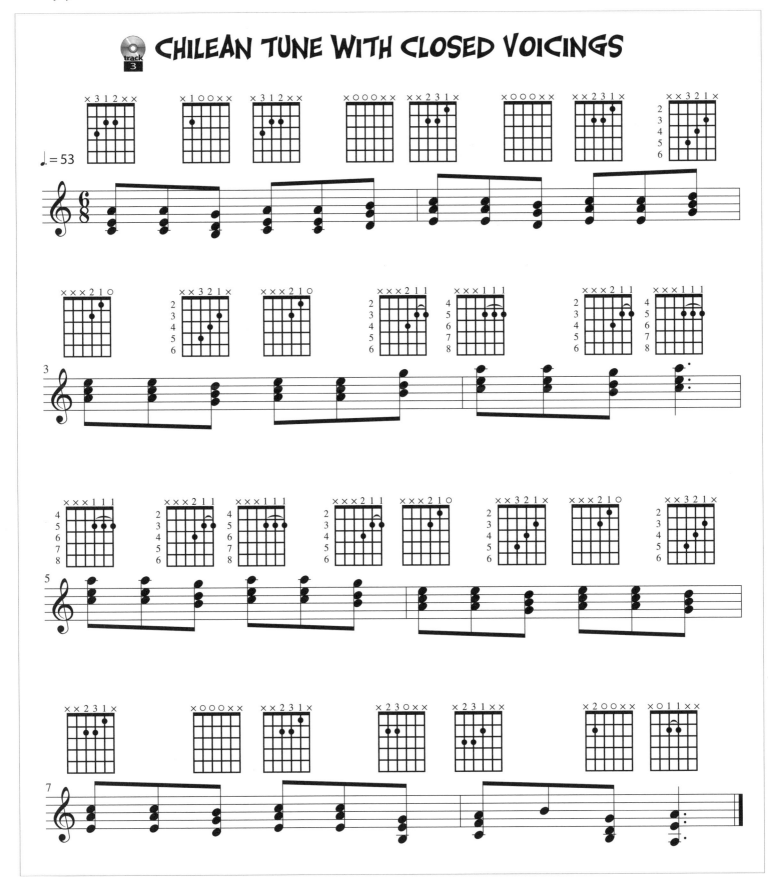

CHILEAN TUNE WITH CLOSED VOICINGS

Practice this until you can see the triad inversions relating to each other.

Now you must use your mind and play the same triads using different fingerings where possible. As an example, below are three different ways to play measures 5 and 6 of *Chilean Tune*. Take your time and think this through.

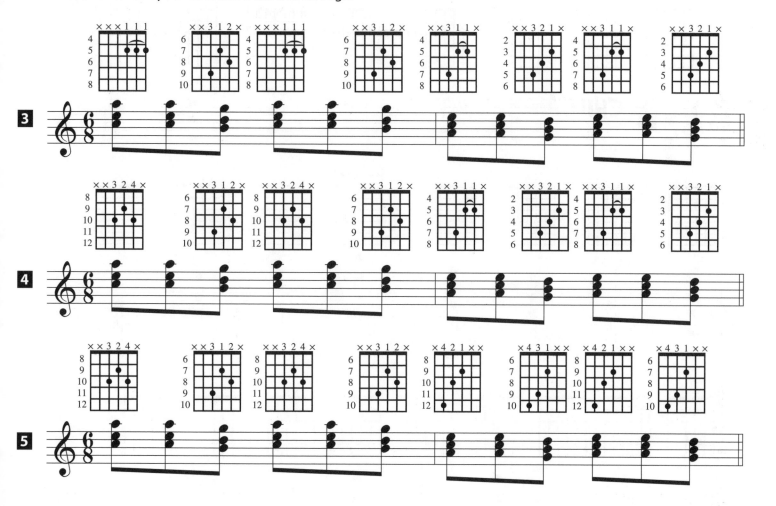

Minor Triads in Open Voicing

Now that we've covered closed A Minor voicings, let's move on to *open voicing* A Minor triads. Open voicing refers to chord voicings in which the notes are spread out over more than an octave.

Here are the three inversions of A Minor in open voicings:

A Minor

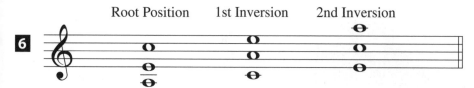

Take a look at example 7. Again, take the time to understand the triads. Don't just play them.

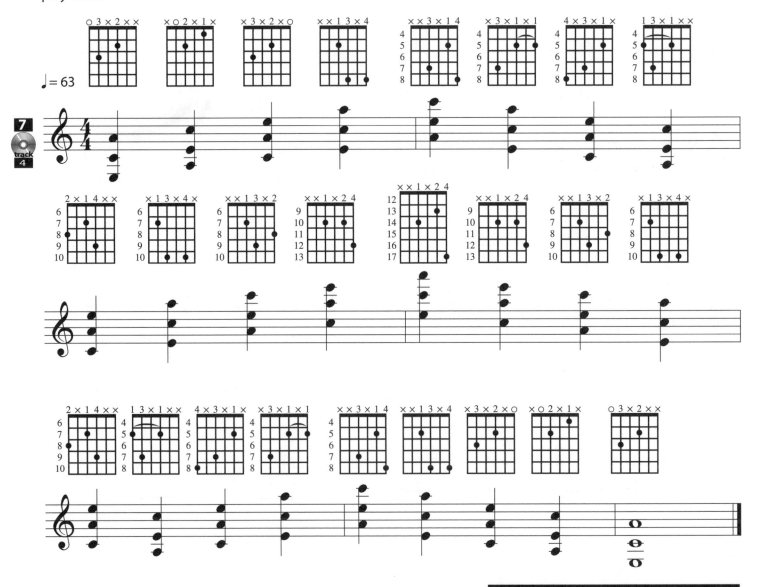

EXTRA STUDY:

Try to play example 7 using A Major triads instead of A Minor.

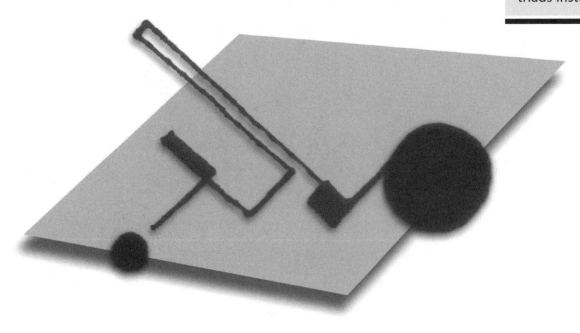

Here's our Chilean-style tune again, this time with open triads.

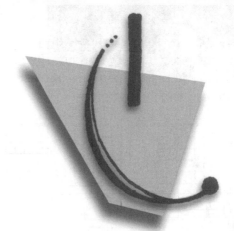

CHILEAN TUNE WITH OPEN VOICINGS

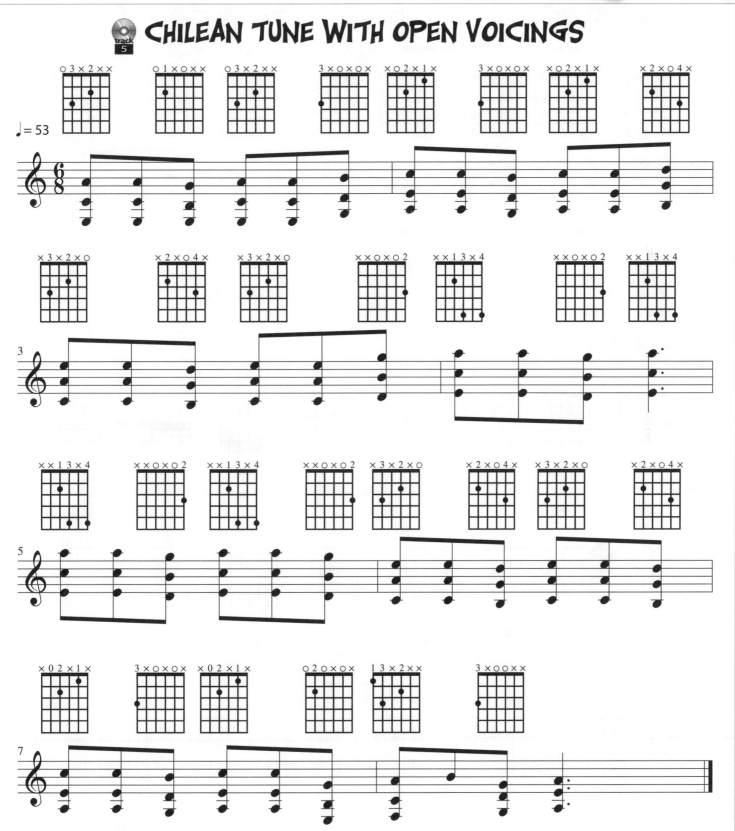

There are several ways to finger the phrases in *Chilean Tune with Open Voicings*, too. Experiment and come up with some alternatives. Work through some different fingerings until you can see the patterns. Here are two alternate choices for triad fingerings for measures 5 and 6 of the piece:

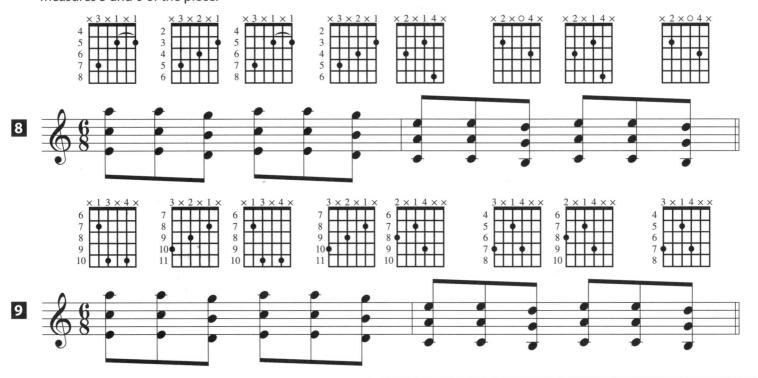

A Triad Tune

Now that we've worked through these exercises with A Minor triads, let's take a look at C Major. I'll give you the same format of closed and open triad exercises below.

Closed Voicing

The first three triads in this example are 2nd position, root position and 1st inversion.

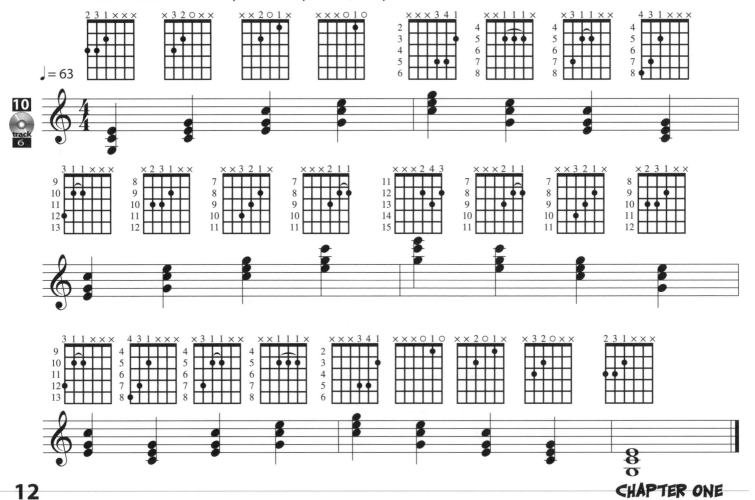

Open Voicing

The first three triads are 1st inversion, 2nd inversion and root position.

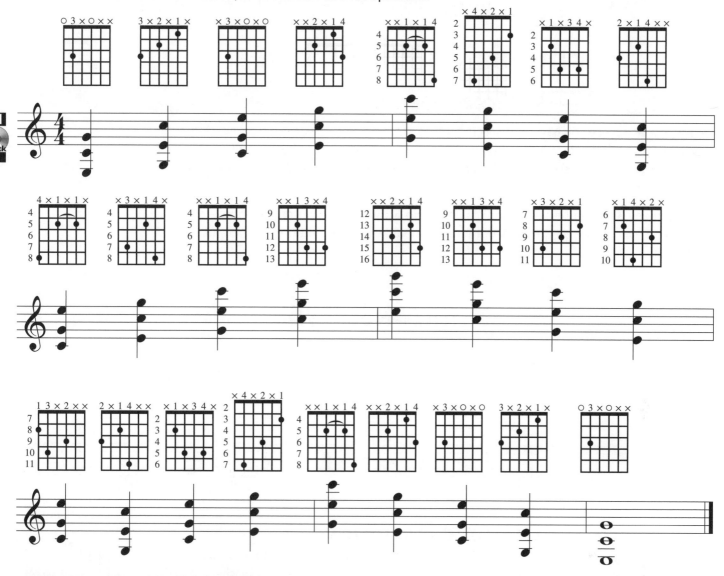

TRIADS

CHAPTER TWO

Harmonizing With Triads

Greensleeves

Let's deal with a piece you have probably heard and played many times, the old English folk song *Greensleeves*. It's important to be able to play a song you have heard by ear, so first we must figure out the melody and chords to the song. Before you read the melody below, see if you can pick it out by ear from memory.

If you hit many wrong notes in trying to play the melody by ear, don't worry. It takes practice. But spend time every day trying to pick out familiar melodies by ear, without the help of printed music. You will improve.

Now, let's read *Greensleeves* from the music.

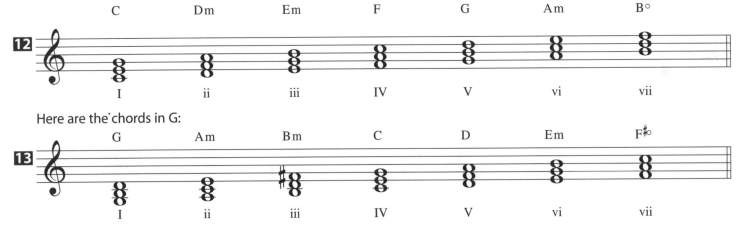

Diatonic Harmony

Now, hum the melody and see if you can find the right chords. When it comes to playing music by ear, this skill is priceless. If this is hard for you, try taking an ear training class or check out *Ear Training for the Conemporary Guitarist*, also published by the National Guitar Workshop and Alfred.

Most of the chords for this tune come from the key of C Major/A Minor, but Renaissance music has a way of being slippery in the key center, so sometimes it can seem like G Major/E Minor. It would be good to remind yourself first of the basic diatonic chords in both C Major/A Minor and G Major/E Minor.

> **Dm = D Minor**
>
> **B∘ = B Diminished**

Here's a quick review of how this works: Build a triad on each note of the major scale using only notes from the scale. Labeling each chord with a Roman numeral (uppercase for major chords and lowercase for minor and diminished), the results will be as follows: I – ii – iii – IV – V – vi – vii∘– I. In C, that's: C Major – D Minor – E Minor – F Major – G Major – A Minor – B Diminished.

Here are the chords in G:

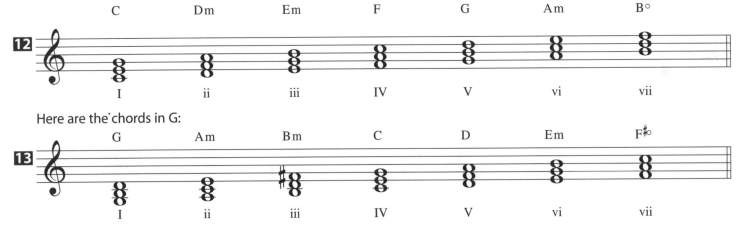

Let's first make a lead sheet for the A section (first section) of *Greensleeves*, so we can see at a glance both the harmony and melody. *Greensleeves* can be harmonized several different ways. In the jazz tradition, it is acceptable and even desirable to come up with interesting re-harmonizations of melodies, so it's okay to differ from the original. Our basic lead sheet for the A section might look like this:

Greensleeves Lead Sheet, A section

Let's experiment with playing the harmony in closed triads under the melody. I'll give you one possible example here; make up some of your own.

Passing Tone Use in Chord/Melody

Notice that in *Greensleeves with Closed Triads,* there are *passing tones* between chords to facilitate playing in this style. In this context, passing tones can be notes of the melody that you don't want to put chords underneath, or they can be notes used to connect chords. Using passing tones is a big part of playing chord/melody. We'll talk about how and when to use them throughout this book. For now, don't be afraid to experiment with passing tones to connect chords when making up your own examples.

Now we can try the same thing with open-voicing triads. Here's an example of *Greensleeves* harmonized with open-voicing triads.

GREENSLEEVES WITH TRIADS IN OPEN VOICING

Open triad voicings are a little trickier to see, but they have a great sound, and come in handy in both chord/melody and in solo guitar improvisation. Knowing the open voicing triads also helps to illuminate the structure of the more extended voicings we'll use later. It's easier to understand altered voicings when you can quickly relate them to the basic unaltered triad voicings.

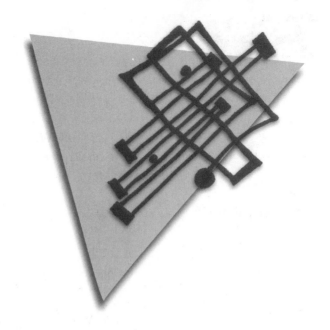

Here's an example of blending open and closed triads to harmonize *Greensleeves*. We are getting more adventurous here, adding some little twists and turns to stir things up. Try your own, and stretch a bit. Have some fun with it.

GREENSLEEVES WITH OPEN AND CLOSED TRIADS

Going Up An Octave

We've been spending time down in first position, but now we need to harmonize *Greensleeves* up an octave, too, using triads in higher positions. For this exercise, first find the triads you need on your own. Take your time, think things through, and look for both open and closed triads between the 5th and 12th frets. Use the melody below, written an octave higher, for reference. Take the time to find these triads. It will help you get a handle on them much quicker if you find them yourself.

Greensleeves Melody One Octave Higher

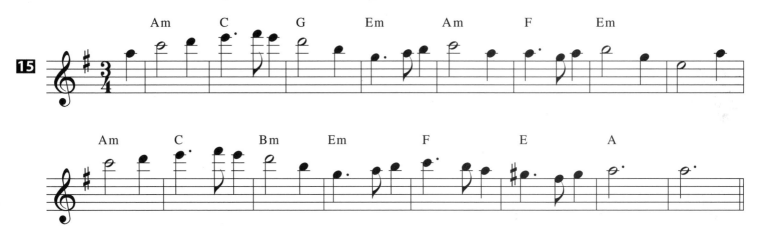

Now that you've done the work finding the triads you need, take a look at this next version of *Greensleeves*. I've moved ahead a little here, and I've begun to put the chord/melody together as more of an arrangement, with extra bass notes and more involved rhythms. Study this example until you can clearly see all the triads.

After you can play this exercise, do two things with it: 1) Say the names of each triad aloud as you play; 2) Write in the chord names, such as "Am," above each chord to help reinforce your grasp of the harmony.

Now, loosen up and fill these blank staves with some versions of your own. You'll notice I haven't supplied you with any B sections for the *Greensleeves* exercises. That's so you can make up your own without any help from me. But feel free to also make up new A sections, too. Don't stay within the rules; feel free to go beyond what we've talked about. Be creative, engage your imagination and get free.

Greensleeves—Extending the Harmonies

When playing jazz we often extend and alter the chords to make them more colorful. Since we worked with the basic triad harmonies in the previous chapter, now we are ready to employ some jazzier chords.

The simplest extensions we could add are the 7th and the 9th. But one must know what kind of 7th or 9th to add. For example, in the second C Major chord in *Greensleeves*, would you add a major 7th or a dominant 7th? A ♭9 or a major 9? Think through the entire A section of *Greensleeves* on your own, and identify what kind of 7th or 9th would be correct (fit in the key) for each chord. It's a little tricky because Renaissance pieces have a way of seeming to shift key centers within a phrase. But no matter; make a guess if you aren't sure, see what that extension sounds like, then try to explain it theoretically. If you need to review some basic theory, now would be a good time to review the first chapter of *Jazz for Classical Cats: Harmony*.

Below is an example liberally sprinkled with extended chords to harmonize *Greensleeves*. Look for lots of major 9 chords, some dominant 7s and minor 7s, as well.

To help you check your work, here is an analysis of the arrangement on page 20.

Now you should be confident as you analyze the next arrangement.

G△9	= G Major 9
Em9	= E minor 9
C△13	= C Major 13
Asus	= A suspended 4th

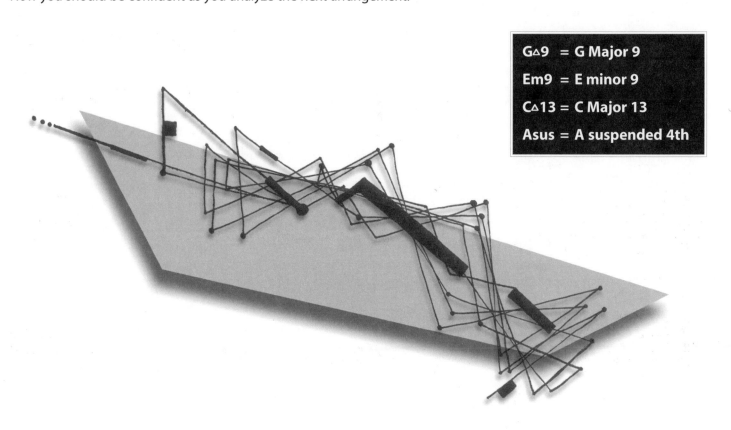

Following is a version of *Greensleeves* in a higher octave. It includes the B section too, so it is complete. I've left the chord diagram boxes blank for you to fill in. Writing and seeing the shape of each chord helps you to assimilate it. Identify every chord and its extensions. Study this example, don't just play it!

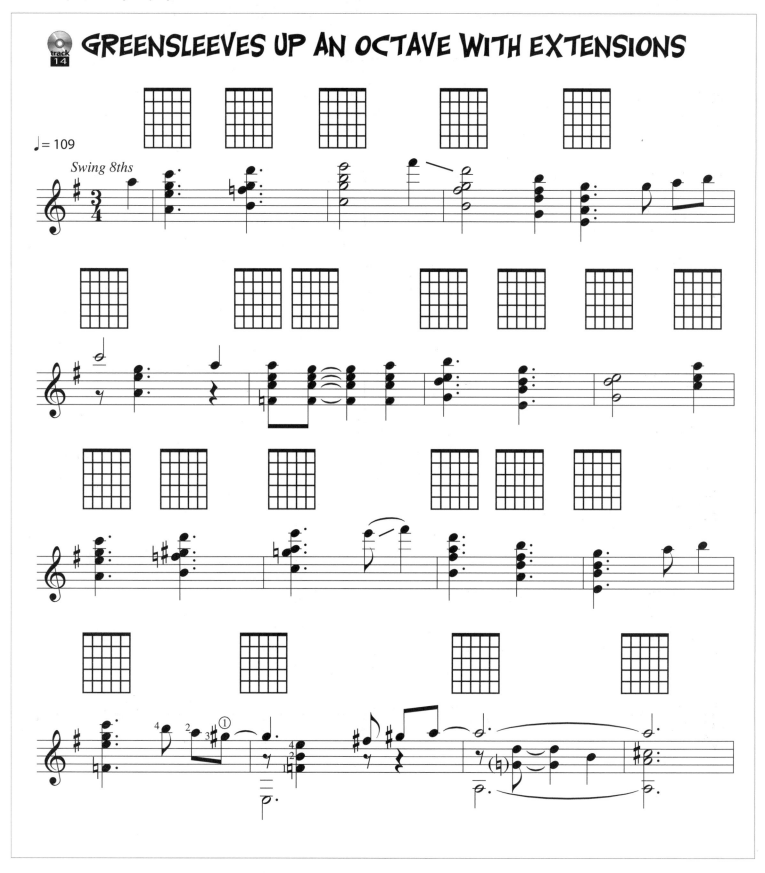

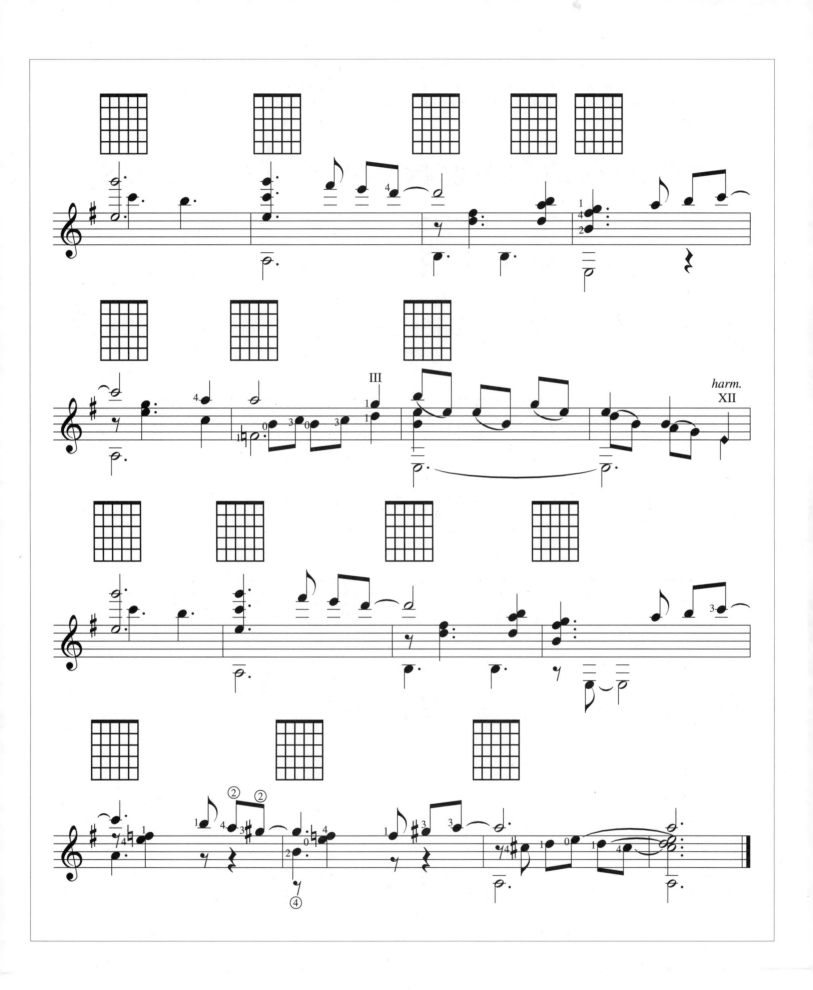

CHAPTER FOUR

Harmonizing Each Note of the Scale

To play chord/melody, you must be able to play a chord underneath any melody note. To learn how to do this, let's practice putting chords under each note of a scale. In this chapter, we'll use a C Major scale and harmonize each note with C (major), Dm and G7 chords. This way we cover ii, V and I, which also gives us minor, major and dominant shapes.

Harmonizing the C Major Scale with a C Major Chord

First, let's cover the 1st string. We'll put all the scale tones on the 1st string, treat them as melody notes and play C Major shapes under each. All the choices I've made for chords are arbitrary—they are easy to grab and will be functional. You can certainly play any C Major-functioning chord you want under each scale tone. Don't be locked in by my example here. You'll notice I freely used C△7, C6 and C⁶₉ chords.

As for the chord under the melody note F, consider that a *passing chord* (one that really doesn't fit the key), since it is a tricky tone to assimilate into a C Major chord. (See next chapter for more on passing tones and passing chords.)

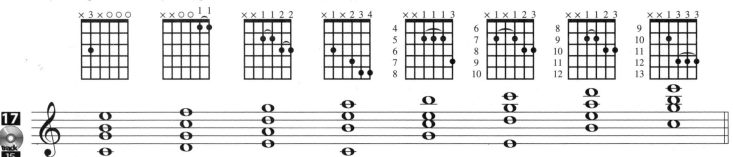

After learning this exercise, use your ear and create little melodies that you can harmonize with these chords. The trick is this: make sure you can "hear" a melody note mentally before you play it. For example, sing the following melody:

♩ = 120*

Make sure you can play the notes correctly by ear, without looking at the music. Then plug in the following chords:

* Many of the ⁴⁄₄ examples on the CD for this book have a click track with only two clicks per measure. These clicks fall on beats 2 and 4 to better communicate the jazz feel.

Now try this by improvising with these chord shapes. Make sure you know which scale/melody tone you are hearing in your mind, so you can play it without fishing for it.

Next we have the C Major notes on the 2nd string, with C Major chords to go under them. The open string B is the 7th degree of the scale, so we'll start there.

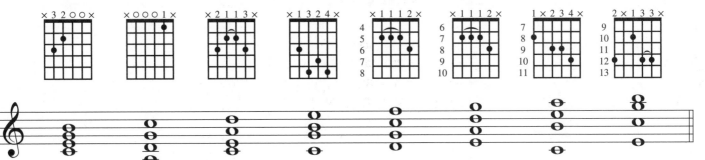

That gives us the C Major scale on both 2nd and 1st strings with C Major chords underneath. Remember that these voicings are arbitrary. Come up with some of your own for each scale tone. Compose a simple melody using both the 1st and 2nd strings, and harmonize them with various C Major chords.

Harmonizing the C Major Scale with G7

Let's go through the same process with G dominant chords, putting various types of G7 chords under each note of the C Major scale. Here are the harmonized scale notes on the 1st string:

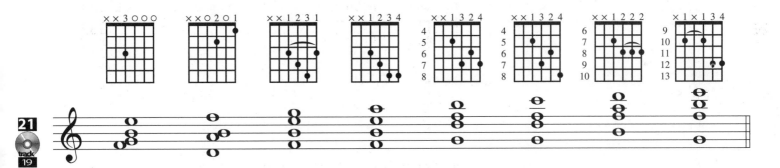

Here is the same thing done with scale tones on the 2nd string:

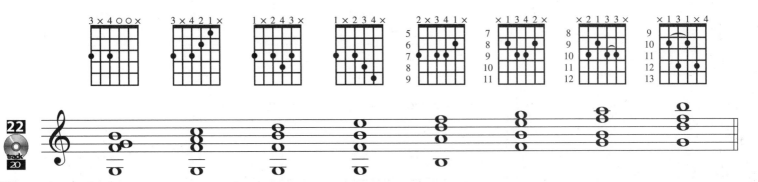

Practice these thoroughly, and try to plug in some different G dominant voicings under the chord tones.

A Sor Study Phrase

Keeping in mind the tonic and dominant chords we just covered, let's look at a phrase from a study by Fernando Sor.

You have probably played this piece. Using some of our C Major scale harmonizations, let's play this jazz chord/melody style. Try it on your own before reading the example below.

You'll notice right away that I changed some of the voicings from those in the earlier examples of scale harmonizations. I even added an altered tone (the A♭ in bar 3). We have to be flexible in jazz and pick voicings that we like and that sound good. Be open to experimenting and doing things freely. Arrange another chord/melody version of the Sor phrase now, and try using some different chord voicings. Think of the different chord voicings as part of your chord vocabulary. The bigger your vocabulary, the better you can express yourself in chord/melody playing.

Harmonizing the C Major Scale with D Minor

Now that we've harmonized the C Major scale with the C Major (I) and G7 (V), we'll finish this set of examples by harmonizing the C Major scale using D Minor (ii). Here is the C Major scale on the 1st string, each note harmonized with a chord that functions as D Minor:

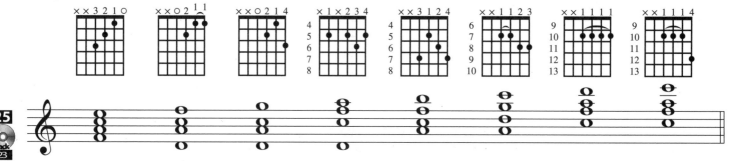

Here it is with scale tones on the 2nd string:

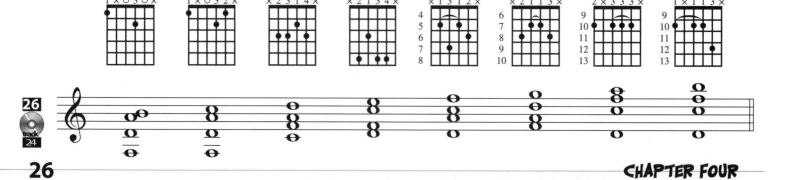

Dominant Chord Chart

We've now used major, dominant and minor chords under scale tones on the 1st and 2nd string. The next exercise puts all three chord functions together, using most of the scale tones. Putting the three chords together results in a IV(ii)–V–I progression (ii is the most common substitute for IV). Playing it with each chord tone on top helps you to play this progression at any point on the neck. This progression is very important in jazz. Study it well.

In the first measure of the exercise below, I've written out a simple swing rhythm, which you can use for the remainder of the exercise. Even though the rest is written in half and whole notes, go ahead and try a little "comping-style" rhythm to add another dimension to this exercise.

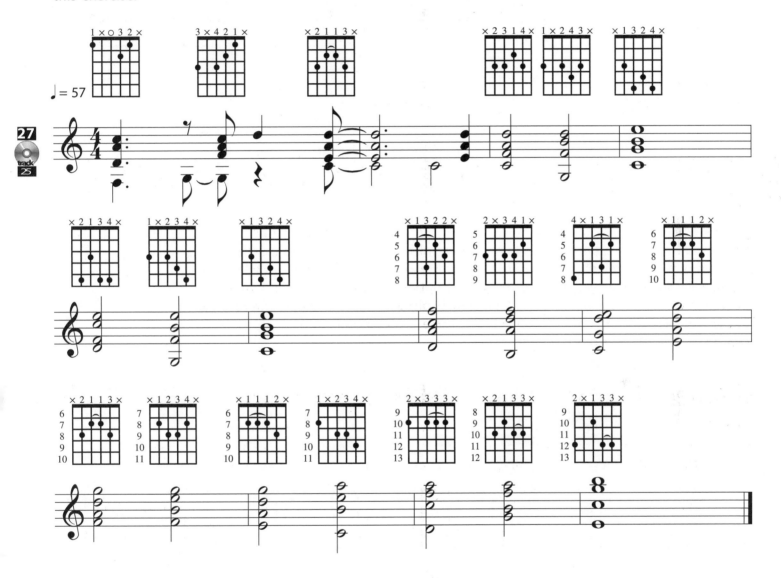

Your next assignment is to do the same type of exercise on your own, this time playing the scale tones on the 1st string. Refer back to the previous examples of the harmonized scale tones and take your time. Working through it carefully yourself will help you master this skill much more quickly in the long run.

Quartal Chords

Quartal chords are simply chords built of stacked 4ths, which are very useful in chord/melody playing. We've used them a lot in this book already. They work very well for harmonizing many of the scale tones, and they make great passing chords. If there is a passing tone in a melody, chances are you can plug in a quartal chord there and it will work. Your ear will be the final judge, but it's amazing how often quartal chords fit right in.

Let's take a look at a simple melody in G Major, with a simple suggested harmony.

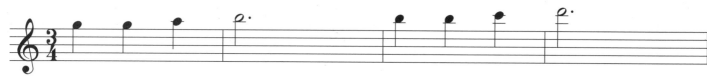

On page 29 are three different ways to harmonize this little melody. Study all three, and notice the use of quartal chords. Some of the chords are only loosely quartel, because one of the intervals in the chord is not a 4th. The examples begin to move away from the use of quartal harmonies in examples 30 and 31, so you can compare the sound and effect of mixing in quartal chords.

Also look for small changes in the harmonic movement. Remember that you don't have to harmonize a melody the same way every time.

ASSIGNMENT:

Write in the names of the chords used for all three examples. Sometimes the choice of names may be ambiguous. That's okay. Make what you think is the most logical guess. The real value here is in studying the chords and analyzing them.

Passing Tones and Deeper Harmony

In this chapter we'll do two things. First, we'll harmonize a short melody three different times, each time making the harmonies more complicated. Second, we'll begin to deal with passing tones in a melody and decide how to harmonize them. Passing tones are melody notes that do not fit into the harmony as they move in a stepwise fashion between the chord tones.

First, here's a simple melody that we'll use as a work subject:

At first glance, we can see it is in E Minor (one sharp in the key signature, and the melody starts and ends on E). But beyond that, we have to decide how we are going to harmonize it.

Using Passing Tones

Since it is very scalar, we'll have to deal with passing tones. When you encounter passing tones in chord/melody playing, you have basically two choices: You can either play the note alone as a passing tone, or you can give it a chord, making it a passing chord.

In example 33, we have taken the simplest approach. The passing tones are played by themselves and the harmonic movement is very basic. This is what you might play if you saw this melody for the first time:

The chords are very simple and intuitive and there are no surprises. This approach sounds good and is a staple of chord/melody playing.

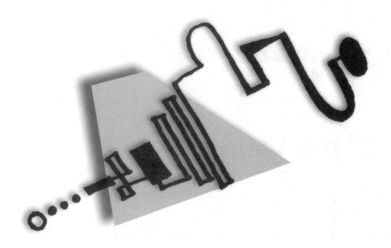

Using Passing Chords

In example 34, the harmony begins to deepen. All the passing tones are now passing chords. Study this example well, and follow the harmonic relationships.

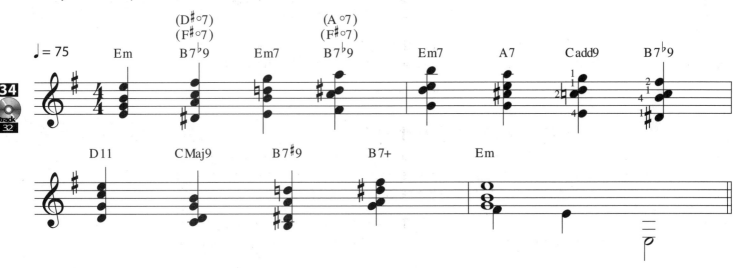

Even though the harmonies sound more complex, almost all of the chords chosen in example are drawn from the E Minor scales (E Natural Minor and E Harmonic Minor). This is true except for the A7, which is a secondary dominant (V of VII). It works well because the chord before it is an Em, and going Em to A7 is like playing ii–V. That, of course, is the most common progression in jazz.

Besides the diminished chords, notice that I've begun to alter the B dominant chords in different ways. There are five different B dominant function chords, and two of them are the diminished 7 chords. The other three are extended with the ♭9, ♯9 and ♯5 (+).

Here is another example with slightly deeper harmonic choices. Spend some time getting to know this one, analyzing the chords and how they fit together and why. Make sure you can identify every chord tone in each chord.

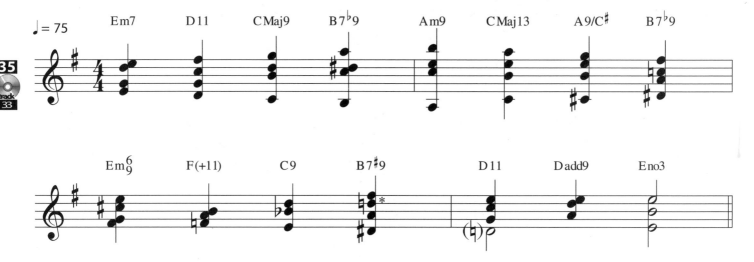

In the first two measures, there is a scalar movement in the bass that moves in contrary motion to the melody. This is fun to play, and since it gives you two notes of each chord already (top and bottom), it helps to define what harmonies and what voicings will be used. In the third and fourth measures, notice the chromatically descending bass line. Making decisions like this involving the bass line can help you find interesting harmonies.

The more you know about harmonic analysis, the better. This will help you understand why some chords work and others sound wrong. But ultimately, your ears tell you what works. The rules help you understand things, but the ears have the final say—even over the rules. If it *sounds* good, then it *is* good. But it is helpful to know why.

Now it's your turn. Make up your own chord/melody version for this example and write it in below.

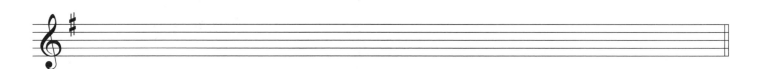

* This B7#9 chord would be more "correctly" spelled with a C* (double sharp), since the 9 of a B dominant chord is C#. In common practice, however, jazz musicians avoid double sharps and double flats, preferring enharmonic respellings for ease of reading.

CHAPTER SIX

Romanza

Romanza, an anonymous piece sometimes called *Spanish Romance*, is one of the most popular classical guitar pieces. Like the exercises in the previous chapter, it has a simple scalar melody in E Minor. Using a familiar tune like this to study chord/melody will teach you a lot about the style.

The Original

Let's take a look at the original *Romanza*. If you don't know this already, learn it now. To avoid a page turn, it starts on page 34.

ROMANZA

Romanza Chord/Melody

Following are two chord/melody versions of this piece for you to study and play. The first chord/ melody version is a duet with a simple repetitive bass line in part two. The rhythm of the melody is significantly changed, but it is all there. There are some different minor and dominant chords for you to check out. The more voicings you know, the more flexibility you'll have in creating chord/melody. Get to know each voicing well, so you can put them in your own vocabulary for chord/melody playing.

Notice how the passing chords come into play here. Usually the harmonization of the passing chord is dominant, creating a pattern of tonic to dominant, as in measures 5 and 6.

I've left off the B section, so your assignment is to create a chord/melody version of the B section yourself. Also, I've left the chord diagram boxes blank above each chord. Fill them in yourself. This will help you retain the chord shapes in your mind.

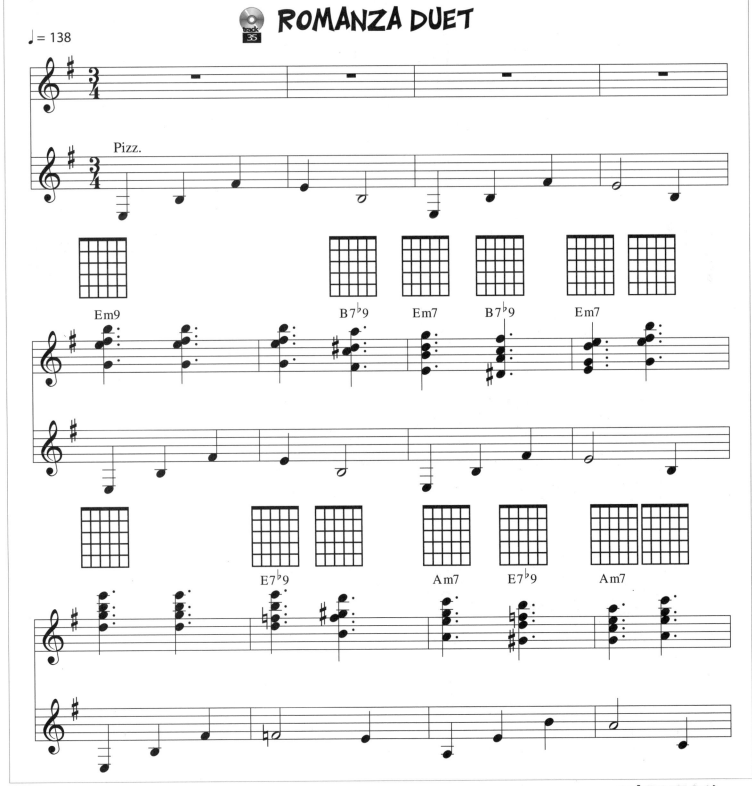

ROMANZA DUET

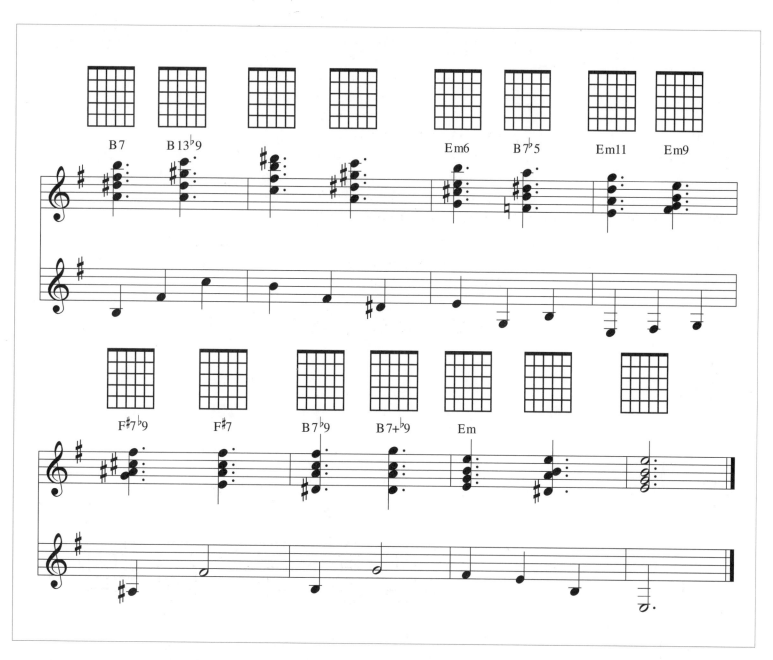

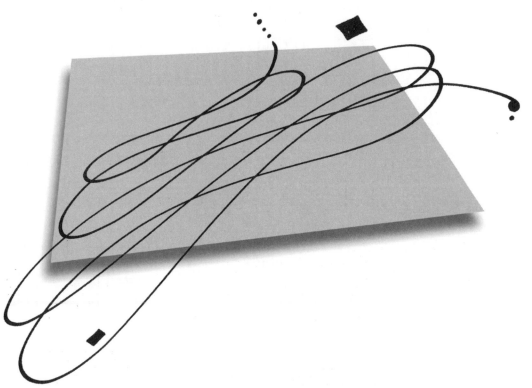

Tritone Substitutions

In the next piece, look out for *tritone substitutions* of the dominant chord. To review, that means the dominant chord can be replaced by a chord a tritone (an interval of three whole steps) away. In this case, and F chord can be used as a substitute for the B7. You'll find this technique used a couple of times. If you analyze the notes, you will see why they can substitute for each other. The distinguishing feature of the dominant chord is the tritone between the 3rd and ♭7th in the chord. It's that tension that makes the chord want to resolve to the tonic (i). The same tones are present in a dominant chord a tritone away. In this case, the tritone notes in the B7 chord are D♯ and A. These notes are also in an F7 chord, although the D♯ is respelled as E♭.

The second chord/melody example of *Romanza* is for solo guitar. I used lots of Em△7 (1–♭3–5–7) and Am△7 chords for a spicier sound in the A section.

The chord forms are in the chord diagram boxes above the music for you to study and learn but the chord names have been left off. Fill them in for each chord (correct answers are provided on page 62–63).

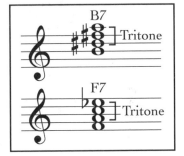

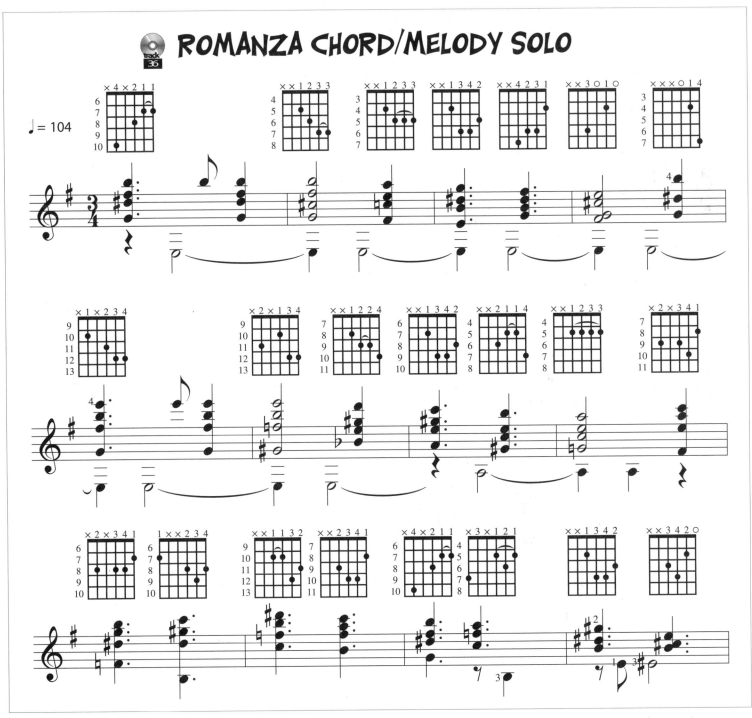

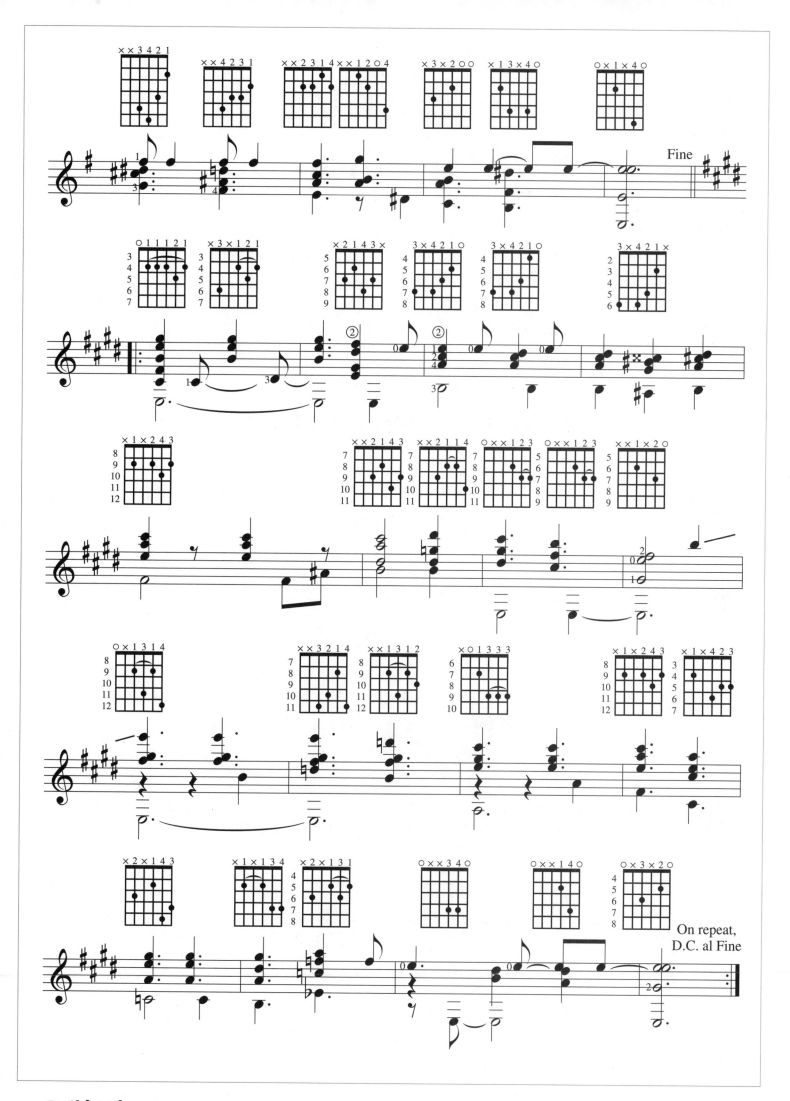

CHAPTER SEVEN

A Few of the Things You Might Be

Chord/melody playing is often based on standard tunes that have been played by jazz players for years. If you study the recordings from the middle of the 20th century to the present, you'll find many of the same tunes represented. We can learn a lot about chord/melody and jazz in general by hearing how different artists realized the same tune.

For this chapter I've chosen the *changes* (chord progression) in the style of a frequently played song, *All the Things You Are,* by Hammerstein and Kern. The melody is completely different, however, and is used as an exercise to practice playing chord/melody over these changes. After learning this version, buy a fake book (hopefully, one of the legal ones, such as *The Real Book*) that includes *All the Things You Are* and make your own chord/melody arrangement of the original.

I've titled this exercise *A Few of the Things You Might Be.* First, let's take a look at a lead-sheet-style chart of the piece, with the melody and basic chord progression.

A FEW OF THE THINGS YOU MIGHT BE—LEAD SHEET

Before learning the chord/melody arrangement of *A Few of the Things You Might Be*, I encourage you to spend a few days experimenting on your own with the lead sheet on page 41 and exploring the possibilities. Remember that it is by making yourself apply new knowledge and thinking through new harmonies that you will learn and grow. Just learning to play what I have written won't take you there; you must work through these concepts yourself.

A Few of the Things You Might Be—Chord/Melody

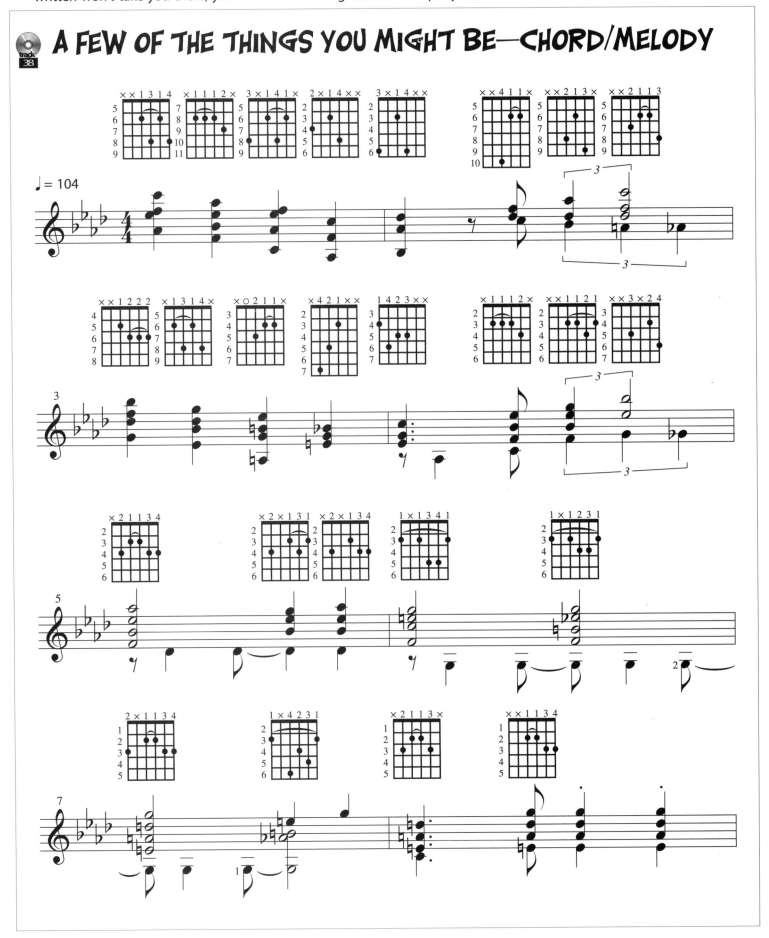

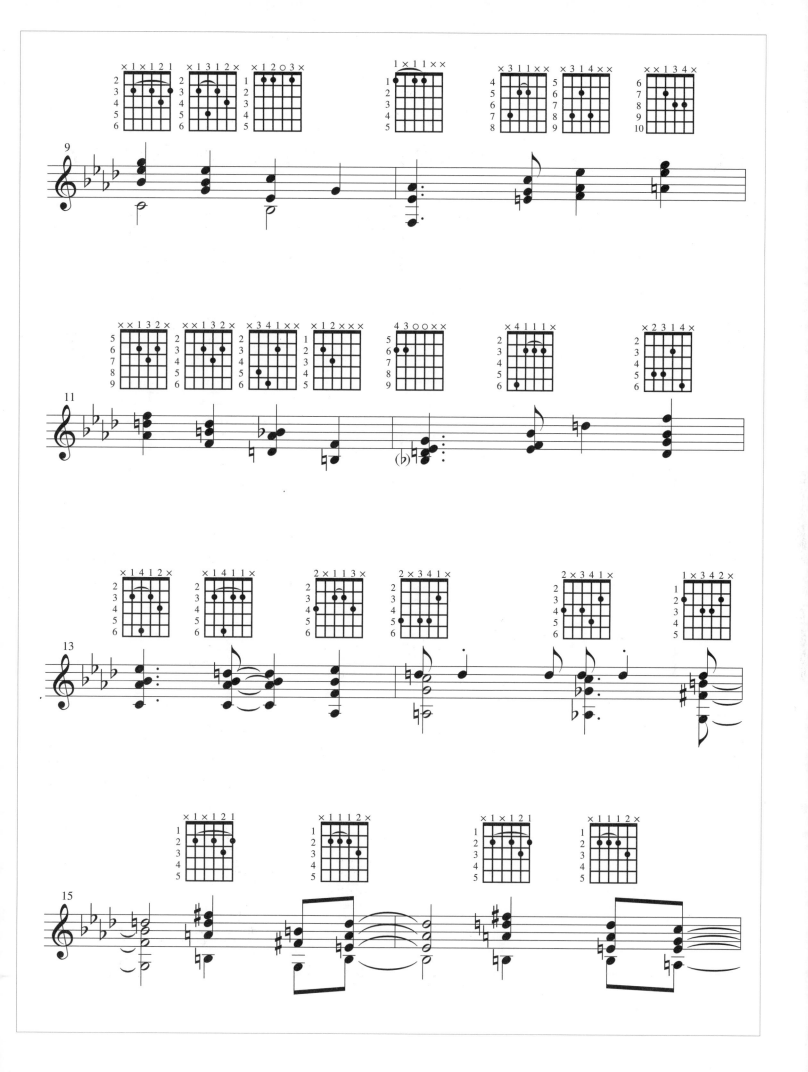

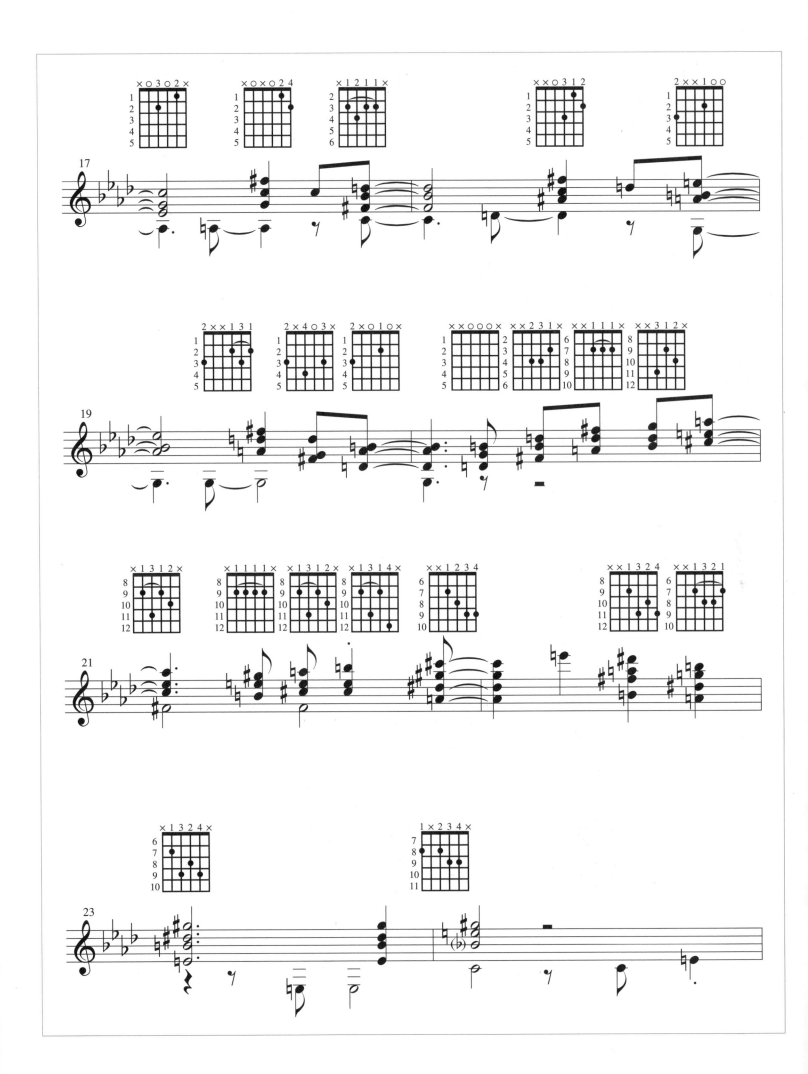

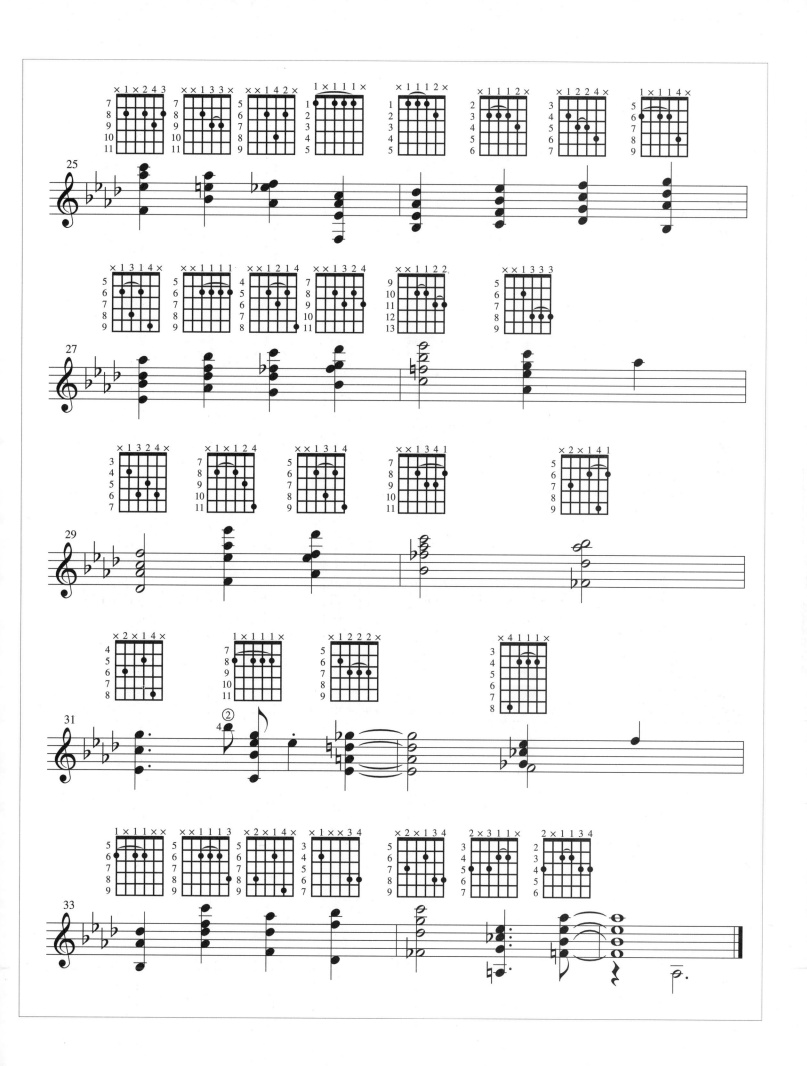

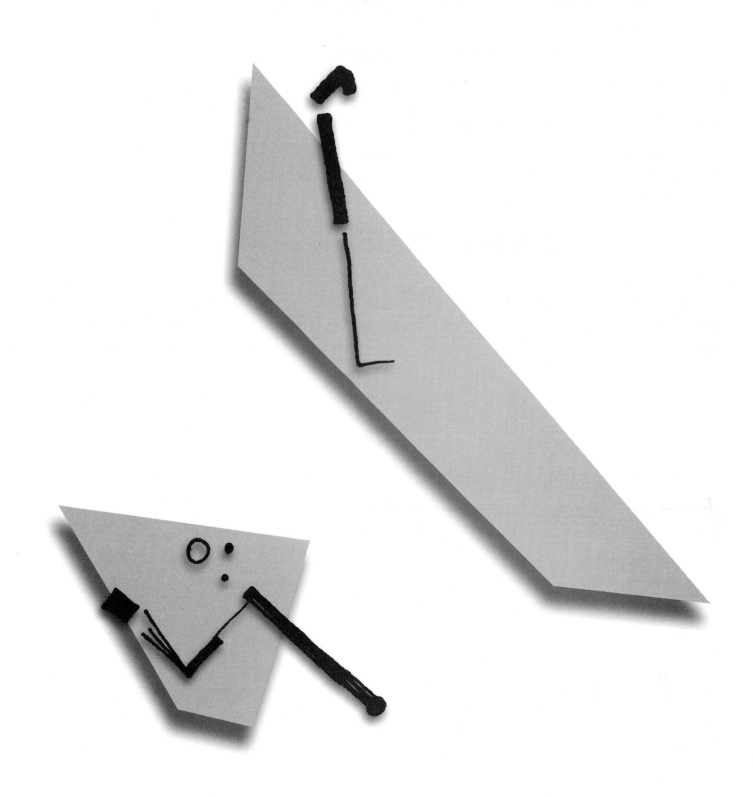

CHAPTER EIGHT
Autumn Sleeves

Autumn Leaves by Johnny Mercer is another famous tune for chord/melody playing. I've taken a basic progression in the style of that tune for the A section and composed a different melody. Check out the original after learning this piece in the style.

As in the last chapter, we'll look at a lead sheet of the song first. Study this for a while, and experiment with voicing the chords yourself before reading the two chord/melody examples I have provided.

Here is a pretty basic chord/melody example of the piece. Study each voicing—don't just memorize the shapes. Analyze them and search for each chord tone. Also notice the inversions. Write in the chord names above each shape. Study them until they become part of your voicing vocabulary. After you can play the piece at a consistent tempo, say each chord name as you play it. Look at your left hand as you do so, and absorb the shapes.

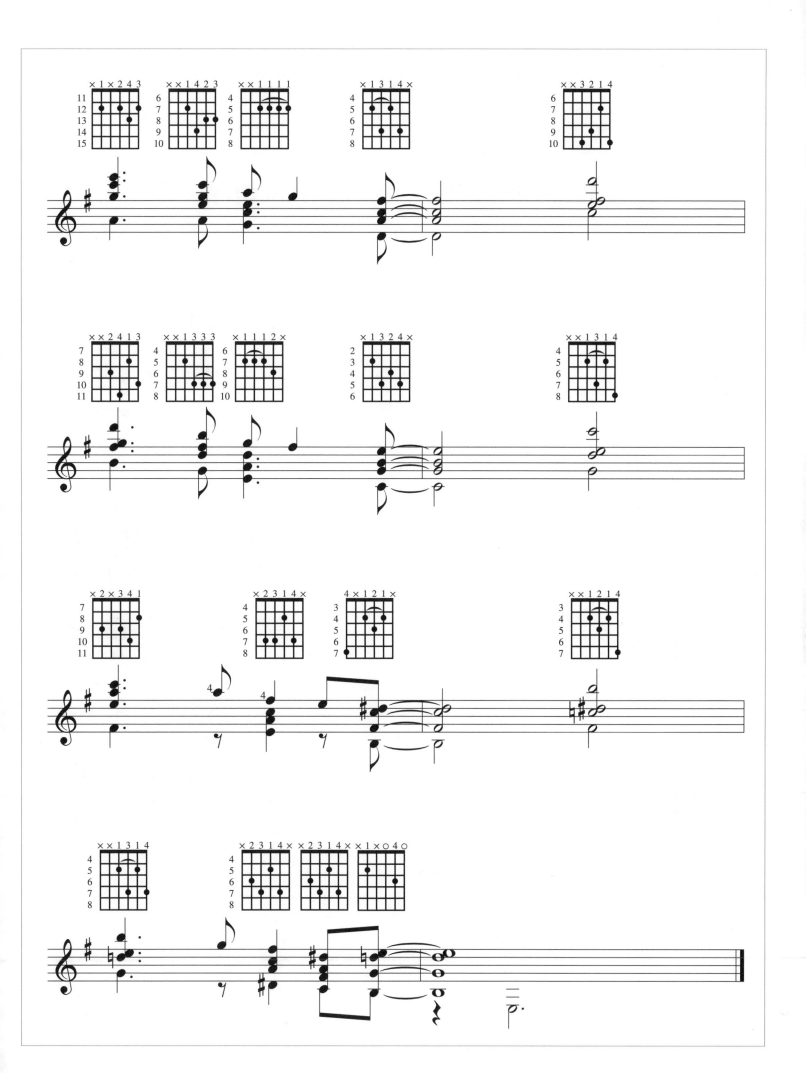

With the second chord/melody setting of this piece, I've gone a little deeper into harmonic choices. Look at the minor chords and watch for the use of both major and minor 7ths. Also study the different choices of bass notes under the chords; there are a few surprising inversions that you should analyze. Again, write in the chord names above the shapes. Take your time, and take apart any unfamiliar voicings note by note and make sure you understand them.

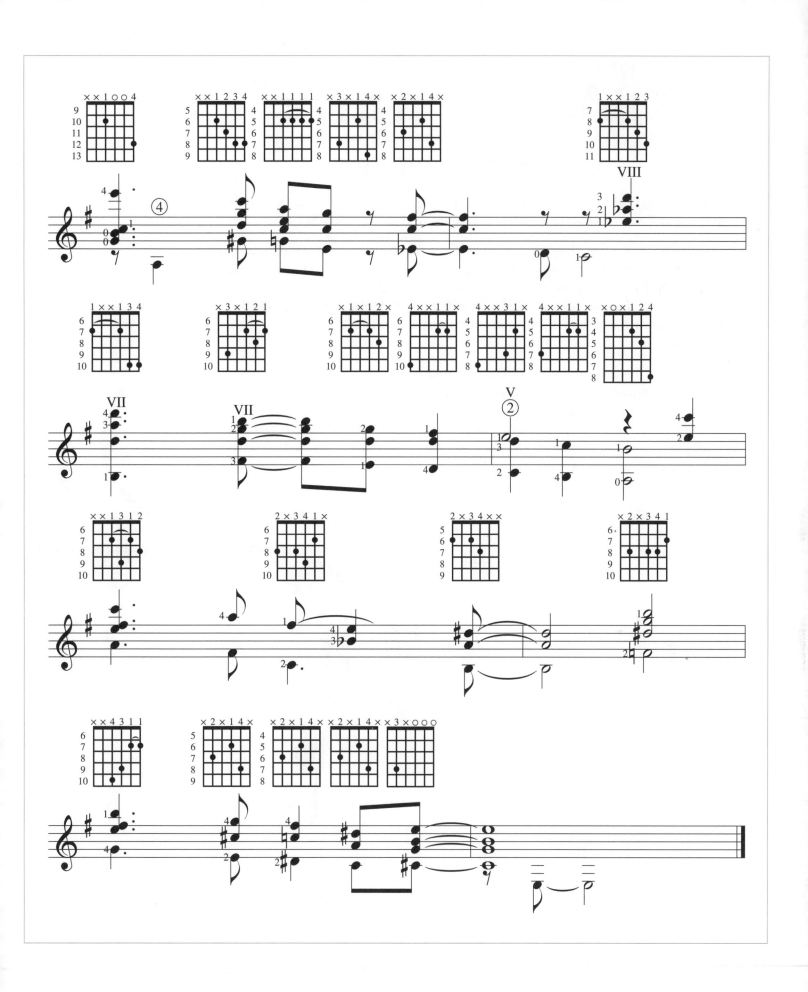

Lagrima de Nuevo

Francisco Tarrega's very sweet and simple piece *Lagrima* is a mainstay in the classical guitar repertoire. I've used it as an exercise to illustrate chord/melody as an arranging skill.

It is useful to be able to play chord/melody style off the top of your head, but it is also important to be able to arrange a chord/melody-style piece. In a way, it is easier to arrange because you have time to think out every measure. But it still takes strong harmony skills and a good imagination. Working out your own arrangements is the best way to build your chord/melody skills; it forces you to analyze your target piece thoroughly and allows you to use new voicings, which deepens your harmonic vocabulary.

Let's first look at the original version of *Lagrima*. Your goal for this piece is to do a harmonic analysis. I recommend that you don't limit yourself to only a traditional harmonic analysis (I–ii–V, etc.). It is fine to write your analysis this way, but also write the chord symbol for each chord (Em7, B7+5, etc.). Then, if you don't already play it, learn it and *see* (visualize) and say the chord names as you play them. You must internalize the harmonic structure so that you know both what chord you are playing and how that chord functions in the piece.

LAGRIMA

Following is a chord/melody arrangement of *Lagrima*. Notice that, besides just extending the harmonies, I've also taken some liberties with the melody. I didn't keep to one type of jazz style; notice how it shifts character a little in certain phrases. When you arrange a piece in chord/melody style, you are free to experiment. You are limited only by your knowledge of harmony and by your imagination.

Study *Lagrima de Nuevo* like you have all the other exercises and write in the chord forms used where I've left the blank boxes. Again, writing them in yourself reinforces your understanding of the shapes you are learning.

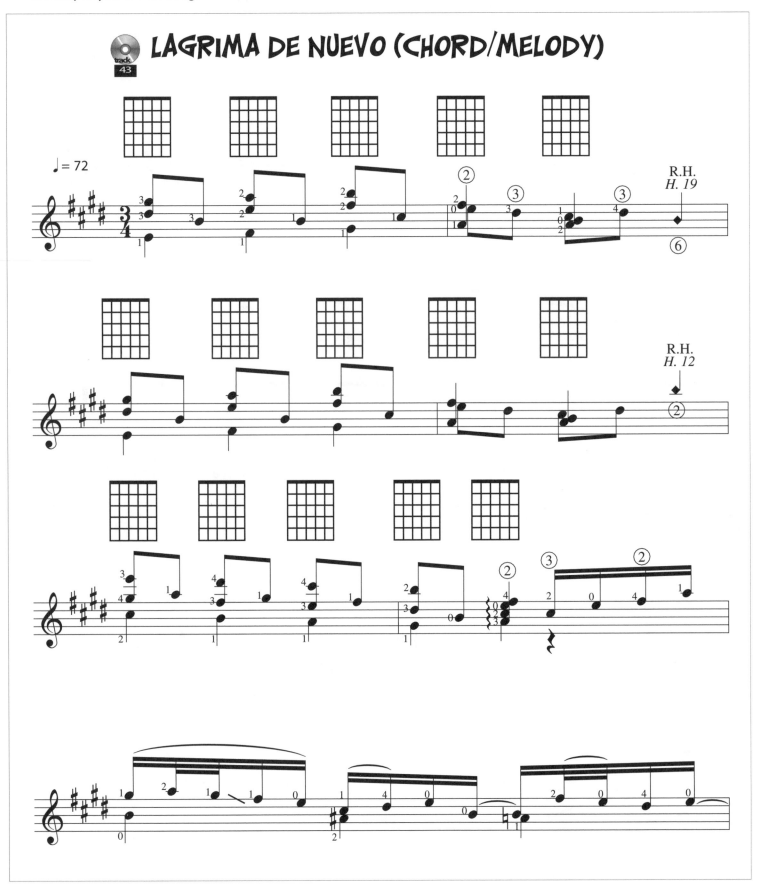

LAGRIMA DE NUEVO (CHORD/MELODY)

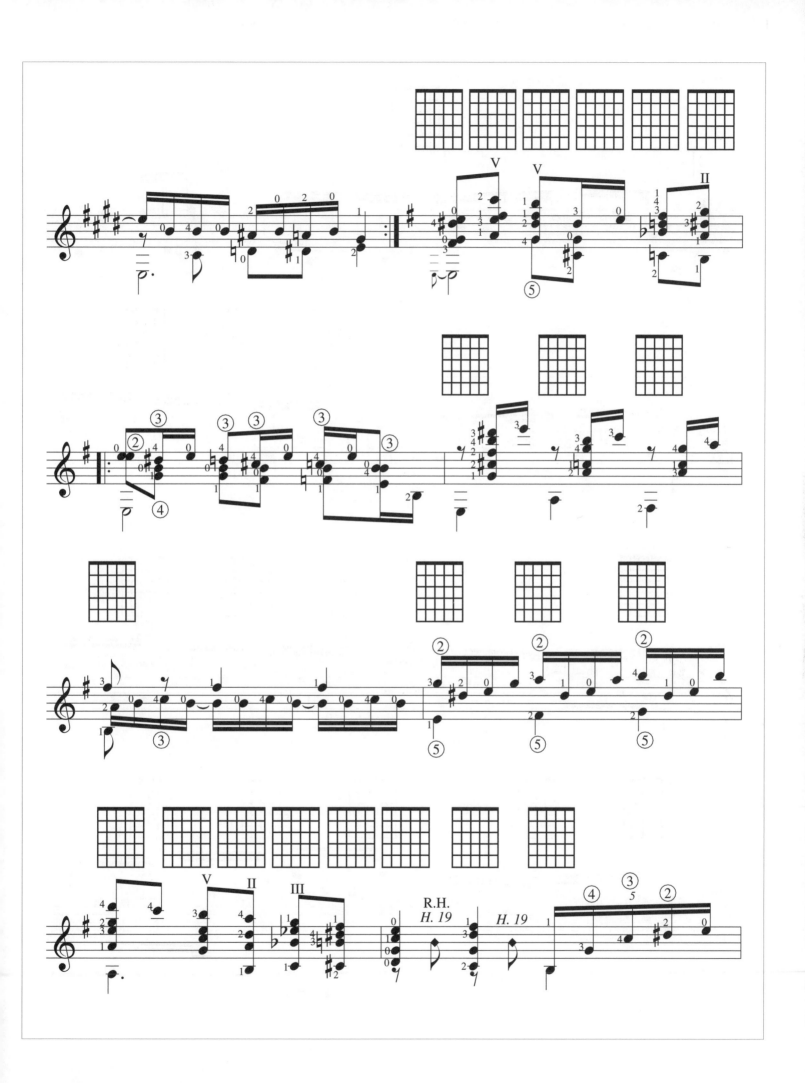

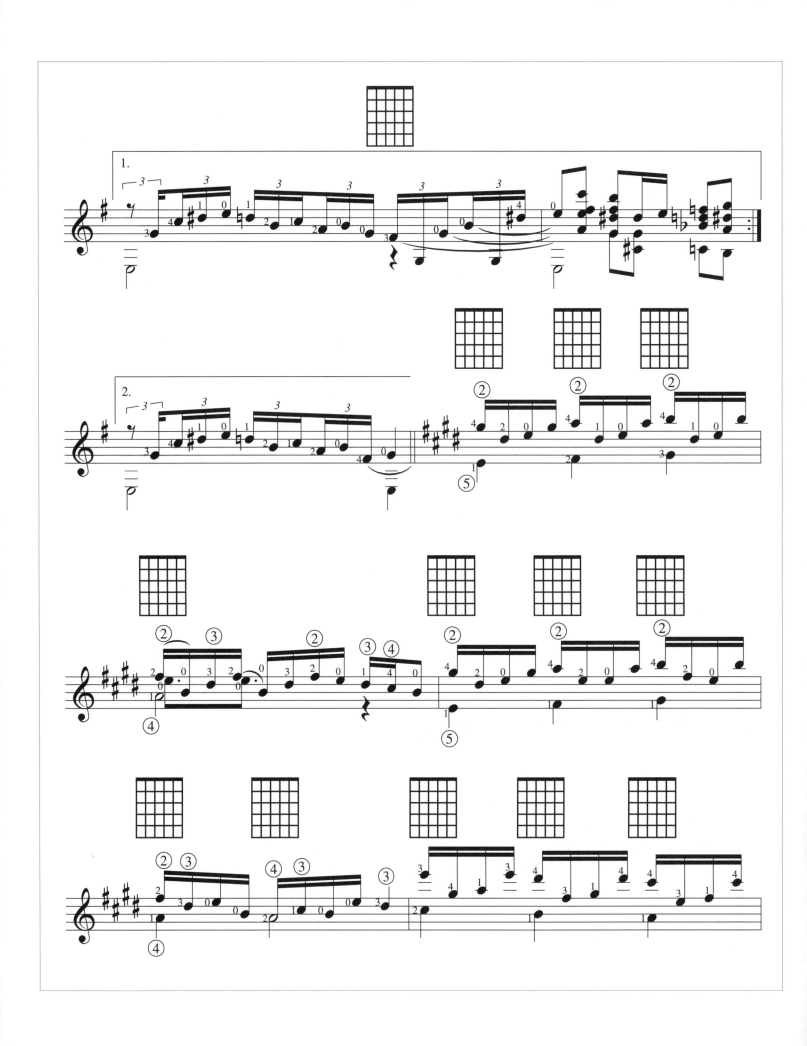

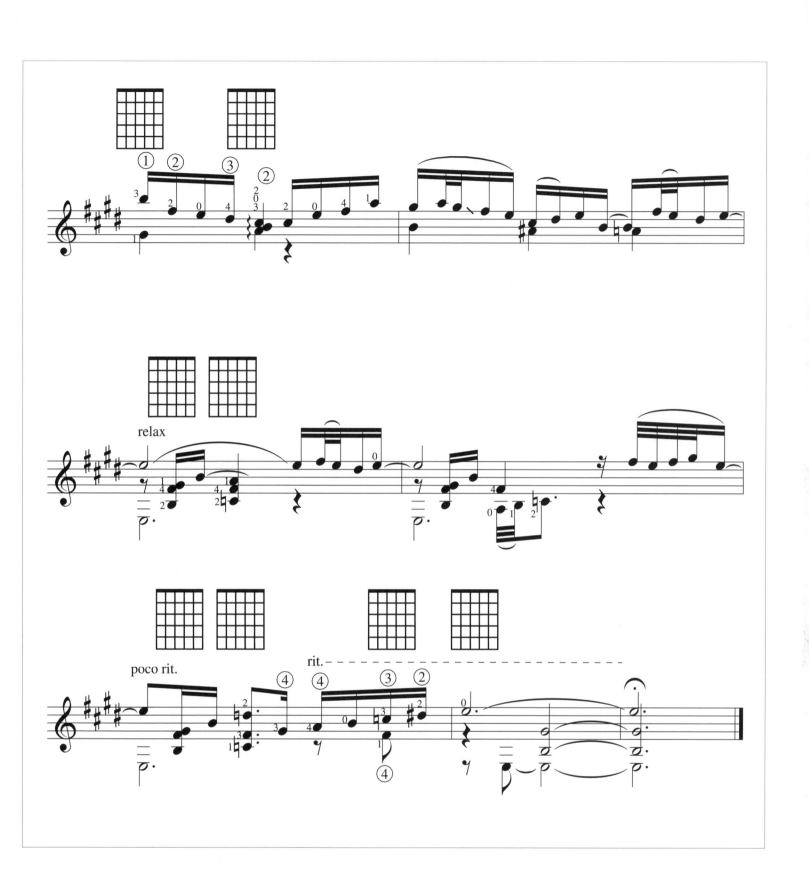

Ode to Joy

Ode to Joy is a very well-known portion of Beethoven's *Ninth Symphony*. Your first exercise here is to listen to the original (if you don't have a good recording of Beethoven's Ninth in your library, get one) and use your ear to do a harmonic analysis. Write down what you hear and see if you can play it on your guitar. Also, fill in the blank chord boxes to learn the voicings.

Always work on developing your ear; that is the most valuable skill you can have as a musician, bar none. Listen to all kinds of music and see if you can catch the harmony by ear. Always practice this—in elevators, bars, shopping malls and at home. Stretch your ears at all times when music is playing and *think* about what you are hearing. This develops your ear.

Here is a little arrangement of *Ode to Joy*. I've stretched the harmony more toward the end. Study it to see how melodic fragments have been reharmonized in different ways as they repeat.

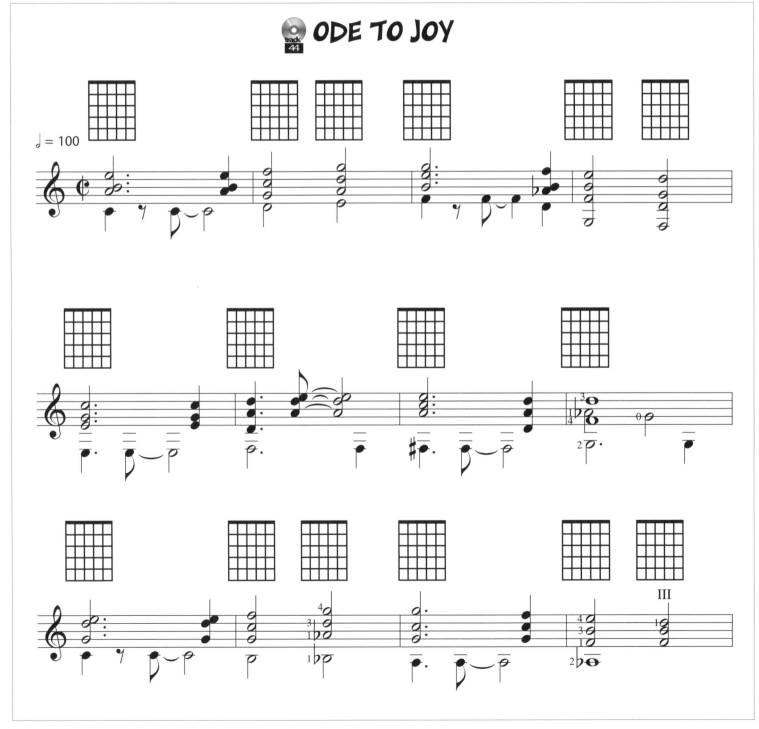

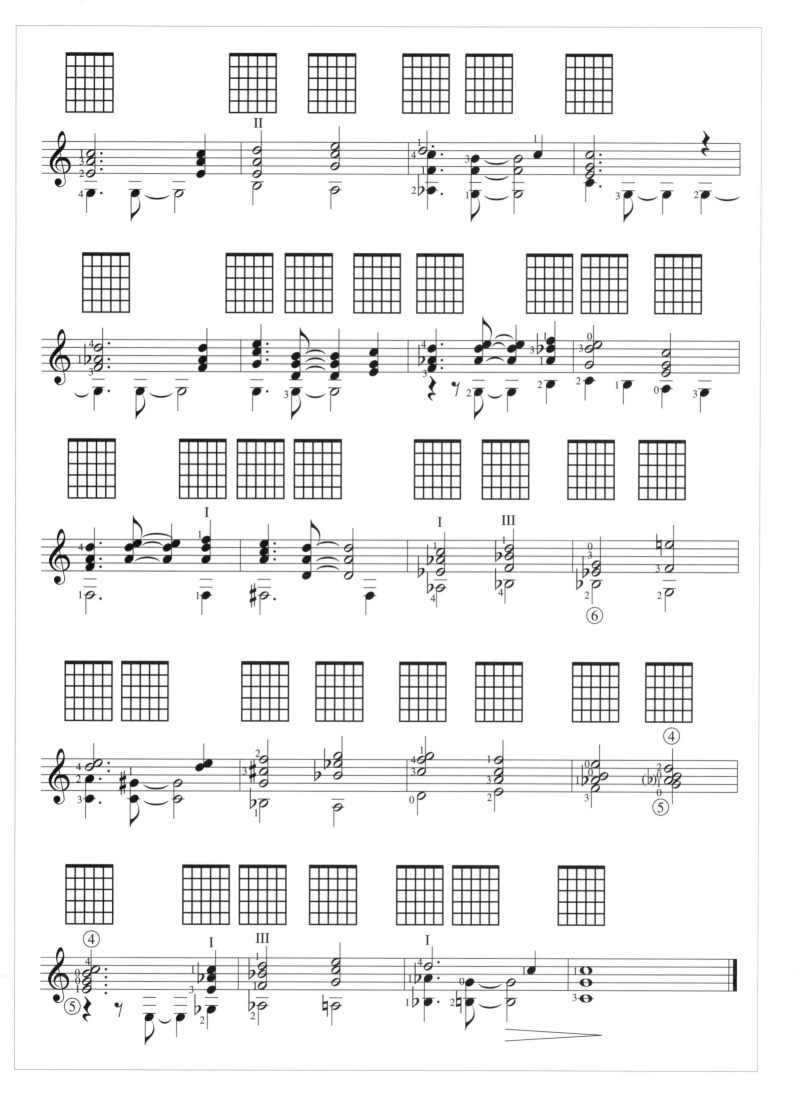

CHAPTER ELEVEN

Blues for J.D.

The final piece in this book is a detailed arrangement of a blues in G. It goes through a twelve-bar blues progression three times. Study how the progression in the composition has been spiced up.

Write the basic blues progression above the staff. For example, above the first measure you would write a "I," and above the second measure a "IV." If you aren't clear on the basic twelve-bar blues progression, you should review it in *Jazz for Classical Cats: Harmony.*

A FINAL WORD

The point of this book has been to help you begin to teach yourself to play chord/melody. You can see that it takes a lot of study and a good knowledge of harmony. You also need a sizeable vocabulary of chord voicings and the understanding to use them. The feeling of being at a loss when confronted with a simple lead sheet will go away as you acquire these skills. Soon, you'll feel the excitement of creating your own chord/melody arrangements.

When getting the pieces in this book up to performance speed, remember what was said at the beginning. Let your classical technique be a strength and not a burden when playing jazz chord/melody. Shift your attitude and play with a lightness and a nimbleness that makes the difficult chord fingering easier. Of course you want to play legato, but when playing chord/melody, we often need to make a friend of shorter articulations. After all, we don't have a sustain pedal to help us out like a pianist does. Wise use of light articulation can make difficult chord/melody passages easier to play, and they'll sound better too.

I have a different mindset when playing jazz than I do when playing classical music. You should also search for a way to think about this material that will make it fresh and manageable to you. You'll find it if you look around the corners of your technique and training, and see where they lead you. Below is the analysis of *Romanza* that was promised on page 38. If you have trouble understanding it, try taking a jazz theory class, or check out *Theory for the Contemporary Guitarist*, also published by the National Guitar Workshop and Alfred. Enjoy each moment in the journey, and you'll pick up new skills every day.